Do You Know Your Worth?

By: Tatiana Whigham

Do You Know Your Worth?
Copyright © 2016 by **Tatiana Whigham**. All rights reserved.

No part of this publication may be reproduced, stored in a retrieval system or transmitted in any way by any means, electronic, mechanical, photocopy, recording or otherwise, without the prior permission of the author except as provided by USA copyright law.

All characters appearing in this work are fictitious. Any resemblance to real persons, living or dead, is purely coincidental.

The opinions expressed by the author are not necessarily those of Revival Waves of Glory Books & Publishing.

Published by Revival Waves of Glory Books & Publishing
PO Box 596| Litchfield, Illinois 62056 USA
www.revivalwavesofgloryministries.com

Revival Waves of Glory Books & Publishing is committed to excellence in the publishing industry.

Book design Copyright © 2016 by Revival Waves of Glory Books & Publishing. All rights reserved.

Published in the United States of America

Paperback: 978-0692702994

Table of Contents

Dedication 4

Author's Notes: 5

Chapter 1: In the Beginning 7

Chapter 2: Accept the Call 17

Chapter 3: In Order to See God's Manifestation, There Must First be Separation! 24

Chapter 4: You're Not a Logo, You're a Brand! 30

Chapter 5: A Diamond in the Rough 37

Chapter 6: Because You're Worth it, Every Problem Serves a Purpose! 40

Other Books By Tatiana Whigham 47

Dedication

This book is dedicated to the wonderful life and memory of my dear uncle.

"Congratulations Evangelist, you finally got your wings!"

December 12, 1958 - August 04, 2015

Author's Notes:

Being a Minister of the Gospel, I get the rare opportunity of meeting people in their most feeble states. It's through these experiences that I've developed a deep sense of duty to using my God-given gifts to encourage the faintest of heart. Often times as I travel in the ministry, I notice how so many people aimlessly shuffle their way through life afraid of taking a step out in faith. They stop believing in the promises of God and stop dreaming of anything better. Seeing this epidemic occur so often in the people of faith, it really began to sadden me.

Our dreams and hopeful expectations are the heartbeats to our sense of motivation. They're the reason why we get up in the morning. They're the reason why we look forward to another day. Without them, even though we're living, we're spiritually dead. Because if we're not believing God for anything, then we unconsciously turn down the abundance of His grace and mercy operating in our lives.

So in writing this piece, I really wanted to get the fact across that if the enemy can make you feel worthless, you'll live faithless! I really hope that you enjoy the book. As always, thanks for your support and God bless!

Chapter 1:
In the Beginning

Then God said, let there be...(Genesis 1:3)

I can recall a story of a young girl. She grew up not having much. Her parents went MIA since before she could remember. Living in a community where nobody really talked about Christ, she grew up with the streets teaching her about life. She fondled through life, never really having a home; and every holiday, she spent it alone. She drifted through school, but eventually dropped out, because she believed that making money was what the world was all about. She was young and very pretty, but early on, she allowed a man to tell her differently. You see, when you grow up without a daddy telling you that you're a queen, you grow up doing all kinds of things. In every man, she searched for affection, ending up night after night jumping from bed to bed without protection. You see, she was using her body to take care of her needs, not really knowing that Jesus came just to set her free. So day after day, she lived in a cage, which was really a glass prison that she herself made. Trapped in depression, low self-esteem, and even doubt, nobody stopped by to tell her that Jesus was the way out. Years went on with drug and alcohol abuse, until she figured out that only the word of God could make one loose.

Who is this girl? She's you, and she's me. She represents everyone who has fallen short in their life. Some of you reading this may say, 'this can never be me.' However, I beg the differ, because my bible tells me that everyone has fallen short of the glory of God (Romans 3:23) and no man is righteous, no not one (Romans 3:10). You see, we're born into sin and shaped into iniquity (Psalms 51:5), this means that without Jesus in our life we could never live right no matter how hard we try. Because to Him, our righteousness is like filthy rags (Isaiah 64:6), we have to come to grips that in God our sins are a thing of the past.

So the first step is realizing that you are not a mistake. When God said, 'Let there be. . .,' He was in the beginning of time thinking of you and me. Jeremiah 1:5 tells us that He knew us before He shaped us in the womb. That means that there is no sin in your life that God did not know about. There is nothing that happens to you that God didn't already foreknow. YOU WERE MADE ON PURPOSE!

This is a big idea, the fact that in the beginning, God was looking through time seeing you and seeing me, and saying, 'My child needs me!' This is a praise moment within itself, realizing that God knew in the beginning of time that you were going to need His help. That's why He said, "Let there be. . . . Let there be light. . . .Let there be darkness (Genesis 1: 2-5). . . ." Speaking on a plainer level, 'Let there be good times, and let there be bad times. This idea is specific to this chapter, because we all need good and bad times to grow.

In the beginning, in the beginning . . . know that everyone's life has a starting point, and know that my starting point does not have to look like yours. Some people started off poor, while others started off rich. Some people grew up in a two parent household, while others grew up in a ditch. Know that everybody is not like you, so everybody won't have the same reactions as you.

By accepting the concept that we all have a beginning, then it is only logical to believe that we all must have an ending. This is a pivotal thought, because it's something that we, ourselves, can control.

Then the man said, "The woman whom You gave to be with me, she gave me of the tree, and I ate."
(Genesis 3: 12)

I love this scripture, because it depicts the world that we live in today: The idea that someone else is responsible or is to blame for our actions. Romans 8:37 tells us that we are more than conquerors. This statement is so powerful, because it's telling us that we have the power to overcome our circumstances. Yes, you may have had a terrible childhood, but that part of your life is over, LET IT GO! Yes, you may have been raped, abused, or mistreated, but that's ok, IT'S OVER NOW! Yes, somebody may have wasted years of your life telling you that they loved you when they didn't, MOVE ON! Yes, you can take it, and yes, you can make it.

In order to grow in God, we have to accept our ability to make decisions. This idea is what I call the 'Seed Theory'. You see, when seeds are planted, a lot of factors play a part in the successful growth of a plant. Soil plays a part. Lighting plays a part. Water plays a part. Space plays a part, and so on. Taking this concept a step further, you see in the natural eye, what you have planted with your spiritual eye. You can't plant seeds of hate in a soil of unforgiveness, watering it daily with old memories and old grudges, and expect to receive a plant of joy, a plant of happiness, or even a plant of love. You SEE what you PLANT!

This is why many young girls who grow up with bad father-daughter relations often times grow up to have trouble keeping or sustaining a positive relationship of their own, because they bring that same hate, that same mistrust, that same negative feeling toward men into their own relationships; and it's unfair to expect a new guy to play 'Captian Saver' and heal old wounds.

1 Corinthians 3: 4-9 talks about the roles that Christians play in the Gospel, 'some water. . . .some plant. . .etc.' It is imperative that we apply the same principles to our lives if we plan to see God's will manifest within us. We have to be determined to plant our life seeds in good grounds. This brings us to the fact that happiness is A CHOICE THAT WE MAKE DAILY! If you're not happy with your life, it's because you don't want to be.

You see, so many people get caught up in the 'IF' factor: If I get this job. . . . .If I get this car. . . If I get this degree. . . then I'll be happy. When in reality, you're using your 'IFs' to be responsible for making you happy. What actually ends up happening is that we get so caught up in the 'IFs,' that we lose the joy of the 'NOW.' Don't miss out on your NOW worried about an IF. Choose to bloom where you're planted. Declare each morning that, 'Today, I don't care what's going on, I'm going to have joy, and I'm going to have peace.' In order to receive, you must first DECLARE and BELIEVE!

Ok, so now that we know that we were made on purpose, and that we can control our 'NOW', it's time to knock off the 'Cain Effect!'

If you do well, will you not be accepted. . .?
(Genesis 4:7)

So two kids were playing outside, a boy and a girl, and they were having a good time. When one would build a sand castle, the other one would too. When one would climb the slide, the other one was right behind him. But halfway through recess, the boy tells the girl, 'I want to race to the pole,' so the girl agrees. They go to the fence and count off, 3. . .2. . .1. . . GO! They start off together. . . passing the rocking horses, still together. . .passing the merry-go-round, still together. . . but when they past the swings, there was a big hole in the ground (because this was the place where they had built their sand castles). The boy falls into the hole, and so does the girl. The boy yells, 'Ouch' and rubs his hurting knee, but the girl dusts herself off, and proceeds to finish the race. Seeing that the girl kept running, the boy gets up and tries his best to catch her. When He realizes that she's pretty far ahead, he walks to the finish line, and she wins the race. The rest of recess, the boy wouldn't even talk to the girl. He actually avoided her. When they went inside and had snack, he sat at another table and picked at her with other children. After school, he took off two minutes early just so he wouldn't have to walk home with her. For the rest of the week, he treated her this way. The next Monday, the kids go outside for recess. One kid with glasses goes to the boy and ask, 'Why don't you play with her anymore.' The boy replies, 'I don't like her. She always cheats. Last week, we were racing, and we fell. But she got up and finished the race before I did.' The kid with glasses looked at the boy for a minute, and then asks him, 'Well, why didn't you get up and run too?' The boy, feeling himself getting angry, replies again, 'But why? What's the use? She was already too far ahead of me.' The kid with the glasses takes a minute and looks at the boy again and says, 'Well, how do you know? You didn't even try.'

As in the story, people are fine with you as long as you do what they do. The boy was fine with the girl when she built castles just like him. The boy was fine with the girl when she went down the slide the same way he did. You see, he didn't have a problem with her until she became different. What I like most about this story is the fact that the boy didn't just fall into hole, the girl did too. But the only difference between them was that the girl did not let that hole (that trouble, that past, that obstacle, or even that setback) hinder her. Instead of nursing her wounds, sitting in a pity party, telling others how much her troubles hurt, she picked up her pain, and she kept it moving. My question for you today is which one are you? The boy (the one who nurses his/her pain) or the girl (the one who says even now, I can make it)? Which one are you?

You see, sometimes we get into these pitfalls of life where we feel as though we are the only ones who have trouble in our lives. But my bible tells me in Ecclesiastes 1:9, that there is nothing new under the sun. In other words, there's nothing new about what you're going through. It's been done before. You're not the first to have lost a loved one. You're not the first to have been laid off. You're not the first to have an incurable illness. You're not the first to be a single parent. YOU'RE NOT THE FIRST!

The reason why I call this a 'Cain Effect' is because in our weakness, we believe falsely that other people are more successful because they have better . . . (it can be better breaks, better circumstances, better finances, or etc.). And because they have better, that's why they're so successful. No, no . . . that's not true. You see, I'm writing this right now to call out the 'Cain spirit' in you, in me, in all of us; and with the power of God that dwells in me, I'm telling you, 'Don't be envious of what someone else has, unless you're willing to do what they did to get it.' You see, Cain and Abel grew up birds of a feather, two by two. Whatever Abel did, Cain wanted to do it to. Cain desired to be accepted by God the same way that Abel was, but he wasn't willing to make the sacrifices that Abel made.

When Cain gave to God, he gave what he had left. Some of you, like Cain, are giving life's dreams what you have left. You'll give your dreams what you have after you buy a house, after you get married, after work, after you have a family, after you go to sleep, after. . after. . .after. And these things are good in themselves, but you can't make your dreams an afterthought and expect them to one day be your reality. Cain gave what was left after the fact, while Abel gave God his best. Abel was chasing a dream to please God and to be the best that he could be. In order to be the best, he had to give the best effort. If you want to get the best out of life, you have to give life your best! If you want to see your dreams come to pass, you have to be willing to sacrifice everything for the dream.

In the Beginning Prayer:

Lord, I thank You for where I am and where I've been.

In my deepest and darkest hour, God, You were there,

And You stayed right by my side.

Please Lord, help me to forgive myself as well as others

For all of the things that may have happened along the way.

I'm so glad Lord, that You made me with both a purpose and a plan.

Lord, please help me to accept the things in life that I cannot change,

And help me to believe and know that You have everything under control.

In Jesus' Name I pray,

Amen.

Chapter 2:
Accept the Call

I can see the sun clear from here, if I can just keep my mind free from fear!

You are significant. You have a purpose in God's kingdom. God didn't just make you, He created you. Knowing this, we are now open to the fact that God has a plan for us, God has a will for us, and yes, God has a mission for us. This epiphany of life having not only a meaning but also a purpose is bewildering to us, because we have to accept the fact that we are worthwhile. We mean something to God. Not that God needs us, but that He actually wants us, and He wants to be a part of our lives.

When I first became serious in my walk with God, I asked Him to give me that sense of more. The 'more' that carried Him to cross. The 'more' that caused Him to love me even when I clearly didn't love myself. More. . .more love. . . more peace. . . more understanding. . . .more selflessness. . . just plain more. And I truly feel that in order to grow in Christ, every Christian must experience that 'more' feeling, that feeling of discontentment with life as is, that feeling of necessary change.

But in a society like the one that we live in today, we are taught that sin is normal. Sex before marriage is normal. Drinking past the point of control is normal. Cursing someone out and blessing God with the same tongue is normal. When sin becomes a habit, change becomes irrelevant. This is why we have said to be Christians, in the church forty or fifty years and doing the same things as the sinner man. If you want to grow in God, you have to be willing to stand out for God.

As you look throughout the bible, people float through life carrying the things that they have learned along the way until God calls them. God's call, even as depicted in scripture, disrupts things. When God called David, it disrupted his life as a shepherd (1 Samuel 16). When God called the disciples, it disrupted their lives as fishermen (Matthew 4:18-22). When God called Paul, it disrupted his life as the elite (Acts 9). When God calls you, your life will be disrupted. God's going to flip your life upside down to trade your plans for His will. In Luke 22:31-32, Jesus tells us that, '. . Satan has asked for you that he may sift you as wheat. But I have prayed for you. . .when you return to me, strengthen your brethren.' In other words, I made it out for a purpose. You made it out for a purpose, and yes, it was worth it!

It's like making a cake. You need your cake mix, eggs, sugar, flour, and etc. You need all these parts to make one cake. Know that flour can't be sweet and sugar can't rise. In plain terms, every ingredient has a role to play, and it's the same with us in the Christian faith. God doesn't call everyone to preach. God doesn't call everyone to sing. When God calls us, we are most effective when we do our God-given role in the Kingdom. 1 Corinthians 12:4-10 explains it best when it speaks of the diversities of God's gifts.

To accept the call,

I realize that I must be changed.

Because when I do so,

My life will never be the same.

God said that He would transform me

From the old to the New

Only then will I see

What I'm truly made to do.

This part of your life is a game changer. You can't just switch up some old habits for a quick fix, because you don't have the power to change yourself by yourself. Isaiah 64:8 explains it best by saying that God is the potter and we are the clay. Don't be afraid to allow God to shape you and to mold you into His image. Now realize that just as the potter has to keep turning the wheel to get the clay just right, God is going to be turning your circumstances, turning your circle of friends, basically turning your life inside out to get you just right. Get this fact, since no one is born saved, we have to go to the potter's house (Jeremiah 18) to learn how to behave. We have to learn how to obey God. We have to learn how to trust God. We have to learn how to love like God. Despite what you believe, love, God's love, does not come naturally. See when we are born, we are taught to show love and affection to those that love us. But realize, not everyone is going to love you like you love them. But when we go to the potter's house and sit down at the wheel, God teaches us that His love is not tied to what we do, His love is not hindered by how well we know one another, ...in order to grow in Christ, His love has to become our love. This is why church is so important. How can you hear the Word of God preached without a preacher (Romans 10:14)? I had a family member tell me once before that he heard God just fine on the TV, and that he didn't need to go to church to be saved because his body is a temple. Yes, your body is a temple, but you can't go through life ministering to yourself if you're lost. You see, you've been ministering to yourself for years and that hasn't gotten you anywhere. It's something about fellowship that grows the strength of the believer. It's just like the game of tag-a-war. By yourself, you're bound to fall, but when you have a number of people pulling with you, it becomes easier to stand. Great minds think alike. You have to surround yourself with people who are on the same path as you. God's love is not a given, it's a gift. When we love God's way, we're not depending on other people to justify why we love them.

Luke 6: 28, tells us that the first step to learning how to love God's way, is to ". . .bless those who curse you, and pray for those who spitefully use you." In order to grasp this, we have to first acknowledge the fact that MISTREAT IS BOUND TO COME! Spoiler alert: YOU WILL BE MISTREATED, but that's alright. YOU WILL BE USED, but that's ok too, because God already said that this would happen. It should come as no surprise. This is why Jesus was able to break bread with Judas knowing that he would betray Him (John 13: 26-28). When you have God's love, it doesn't matter what someone else does to you, because you'll trust God to take care of you!

Putting on the 'New Man' in God is not a onetime decision, it's a daily commitment. This is a cross that we're carrying on a daily basis (Luke 9:23). It's a daily struggle not a quick fix. So being molded and shaped into God's image takes TIME! So when you accept God's call in your life, don't disappoint yourself by expecting to get everything right the first time, you're not perfect; no man is. You will make a mistake, that's a fact. In 1 Samuel 12: 20-21, Samuel explains it best by saying that even though you may have sinned, you should by no means stop pursuing God. When you turn from God because of the embarrassment of your sins, you're opening the door for the enemy to deceive you, because nothing (no alcohol, no drugs, no man, no woman, nothing) can fill the void within you where God is supposed to dwell. So what should you say to this, 'Every man sins, so sin is ok?' NO, certainly not! When growing in Christ, you should avoid any sin that sets you back at all cost (Hebrews 12:1), because from the moment that you accept your call in Christ, you will be surrounded by a cloud of witnesses (Hebrews 12:1) desperately trying to find fault in you on a regular basis.

Prayer for Accepting God's Call

Dear Lord,

Please help me to see the good and perfect will

That you have for my life

Even if it frightens me.

Lord, I want so bad to be close to you.

Here I am Lord,

Visit me just as I am.

Shape me Lord,

Mold me Lord,

Into what you would have me to be.

You are the potter God,

And I am finally ready to be your clay.

Please Lord, guide me along the way.

In Jesus' name,

Amen

Chapter 3:
In Order to See God's Manifestation, There Must First be Separation!

When I was a child, my father used to raise dogs. He'd buy them; breed them, and eventually sell the offspring. One year, I'll never forget it; he surprised me with a dog on my birthday. She was a pretty auburn-brown pit-bull. She was so small, I named her Pebbles. Pebbles grew to be a rather playful puppy. I loved her a lot. She was the last of three puppies for that year. We had two boys (Poochi and Taz) and one girl (Pebbles). A little more than a year or so down the road, I was just getting out of school, and it was custom for me to go outside and let Pebbles into the house. That day, I went to the backdoor and called for her, but she didn't come. At the time, we had a small backyard, so I could see her sitting down just watching me call her like a fool. When she still did not come, I went out to her to bring her in. But instead of coming inside, she snapped at me, got up, and moved to the other side of the fence. Since she had never acted this way before, I went inside and left her alone. When my dad got home,

I told him about how Pebbles behaved that day. I told him that she might be sick or something and that he should go check on her. So, my dad went outside. A few minutes later, he came back in smiling from ear to ear. I ran to him and asked him whether or not Pebbles would be alright. He told me that she was fine, she was just pregnant and that it would be best for me to leave her alone until after she had the puppies. I was thrilled that my dog was about to have puppies and so I did as my dad had instructed.

Just like Pebbles, we go through life just as playful as can be, looking for things to please our wants and desires daily. But when God calls us, we become pregnant just like Mary (Matthew 1:18) with the Holy Spirit. When the Holy Spirit gets on the inside of you, you will receive power (Acts 1:8). This power will comfort you; correct you, discipline you, and direct you into the paths of righteousness (John 16: 5-11). When you're pregnant with the Holy Spirit, separation comes into play. Just like Pebbles stopped coming in and doing the things that she used to do, you will stop doing things that you normally do. You see, nobody will have to tell you, the Spirit of God will convict you. You won't go to the places that you used to go, because the Holy Spirit has the power to make you feel uncomfortable. You won't dress the way that you used to dress, because the Holy Spirit checks its appearance. You won't do the things that you used to do, because the Holy Spirit will cleanse you. That's why Jesus called it the 'Helper,' because He knew that we were going to need a piece of Him daily just to make it through this life. When the spirit gets inside of you, you'll put the Jack Daniel down. When the spirit gets inside of you, you'll leave the drug house. When the spirit gets inside of you, you'll stop settling for less and start picking up your standards. When the spirit gets inside of you, you'll stop shacking up with your boyfriend or girlfriend. When the spirit gets inside of you, it'll teach you how to treat your neighbors. . When the spirit gets inside of you, you'll know how to love the right way. When the spirit gets inside of you, it's going to move some things out of your way. It's going to remove some friends. It's going to remove some hangouts. It's going to remove some thoughts. It's going to remove some pleasures. The spirit of God has the power to change a man from the inside out.

To see God manifest in your life, the Holy Spirit will have to separate you from some things. Since we are not born saved, we have to be taught how to live a saved life. But the problem today, is that there are far too many said to be Christians trying to bring the world into the Church. God is consistent: He was, He is, and He will be (John 1:1). God doesn't change to fit us, we change to fit Him. That's why we're in the world, but not of the world (Romans 12:2), because if we do what the world does, the world will not change. But if we stick out like a city sitting on a hill (Matthew 5:14), things will change. You have to be willing to separate.

When you're pregnant with the Holy Spirit, you have to be in constant communication with God, because the Spirit will reveal what it hears from God (John 16:13). This brings me to my next point!

When prayer becomes a habit, success becomes your friend.

Growing as a Christian, a true follower of Christ is a process, and the process hurts. It's not going to feel good to have your life altered, but it's necessary. It's like a woman delivering a child for the first time. After all of the pain, joy comes. So you have to keep reminding yourself that you have to go through some things to get to the good part. God has to become a friend not a distant relative. God has to become your leaning post, your rock, your everything. When you give your life to Christ, you have to work on falling in love with Him every day of your life. How can you follow someone that you don't talk to? How can you love someone that you never come around?

This thought is baffling because most people view prayer like an incident report. Look God, this is what happened today, blah. . .blah . . .blah. When really, prayer is supposed to be you working your faith. By doing this, you pray believing that God is going to move on your behalf. You'll stop praying about the magnitude of your situation and start telling your situation the magnitude of your God. A lot of times, we treat God like He can handle some things but can't handle others. I don't know about you, but if I'm going to serve a God, I want to be able to believe that He can work things out. I don't serve a part-time God. I serve a God that is always on the scene. When you communicate with God, you tap into the spiritual realm. When you communicate with God in prayer, chains are broken, yokes are destroyed, and you begin to turn your situation around by activating your faith which is your confidence in God.

When you build up your prayer life, which is your communication with God, you become planted and deeply rooted in your faith and not as easily moved by circumstances. Your faith will reflect the fact that God is constant and unchanging. By doing this, you'll develop the 'Winner Syndrome,' which states that I can get through this because the victory is mine, and I can take it because Jesus already made it. The 'Winner Syndrome' gives you a positive attitude on life which enables you to reach greater heights. That's why we are more than conquerors in Jesus (Romans 8:37).

Prayer for God's Manifestation:

Dear Lord,

I thank You for taking the time to work in my life.

I thank You God for being God all by yourself.

And Lord as I go through this life,

Please Lord, talk to me,

Walk with me,

Comfort me along the way,

Be my friend,

My constant provider,

And my counsel.

Lord work on me from the inside out.

In Jesus' name,

Amen.

Chapter 4:
You're Not a Logo, You're a Brand!

One of my favorite dishes to eat is homemade macaroni and cheese. Sadly, my mom doesn't make it but twice a year, that's Thanksgiving and Christmas. So, in the midst of one of my cravings, I decided to attempt to make the dish myself. I rushed to the store with my mom's recipe, grabbing every item on the list. When I got to my house, I couldn't wait to get started. I boiled the noodles, drained them, made the sauce, and now, it was time to add the cheese. I love macaroni with extra cheese, so I purposely bought a pack of cheese with well over 72 slices. But as I began to put the cheese on top of the noodles, there was a problem. No matter how much cheese that I put in the pan, the cheese wouldn't melt. Frantic, I didn't know what to do. But with every minute wasted, my noodles were on the verge of burning. So being out of options, I found some shredded Kraft cheese in the refrigerator. I dumped the whole bag into the pan. Sad and disappointed, instead of the glorious dinner that I had planned, I had fried chicken and burnt macaroni. The next day, my mom called and asked how the macaroni turned out. Still holding the burden of defeat, I didn't want to tell her, but I did. After listening carefully, my mom told me to go over my list of ingredients. I did. After another long pause, she asked me to go over the brand names of each ingredient. I did. After hearing my answer, my mom burst out laughing and said, "Baby, you can't buy No-brand foods for everything." Confused, I asked her what she meant by that. She informed me that I had used the wrong brand of cheese. Still confused, I told my mom that I thought cheese was cheese. Again, she burst out laughing, and said, "Yes, cheese is cheese, but not every cheese melts. Some brands do better than others. That's why I cook with the brands I trust."

That day, I learned the first rule of cooking 101, the quality of foods outweigh the symbols of them. See I thought that just because the list said cheese, any brand of cheese would do, so I got the cheapest brand of cheese that I could find. This same principle applies to the Christian faith. Many people think that in order to be a Christian, they have to look like one. You know with the nice suits, name brand shoes, cross around the neck, and bibles in their hands. I'm sorry to disappoint you, but you can't WEAR the Christian faith, you have to LIVE it!

This is the problem that the Pharisees had with Jesus. They were expecting to see a king, a rich man, or a said to be important man. But what they got was a carpenter working for a few pennies an hour living in the cities slumps. That's like having the pastor of a church living in the projects. When really, the point that Jesus was trying to get across was that it's ok to be successful, but don't let success have you.

It kills me to see said to be Christians become 'overboard Evangelists.' Yes, we are called to spread the gospel, but so many people are only spreading the news with their words. In a world with so much pain, people don't need to HEAR church, they need to SEE church! Stop being the 'Logo Christian' (the one who professes Christ, but can't live it) and start being the 'Brand Christian' (the one who admits his/her fault but seeks God's power to live a righteous life).

God's not asking you to sell Him, He's asking you to be Him: to walk like Him, to talk like Him, to serve like Him, to behave like Him. We are called to put on Christ daily, not to lay Him down when we want to like an accessory. God doesn't want to add to us, He wants to live through us.

You're not a logo; you're a brand. You're not a symbol; you're it. When people think of Christ, they should think of you. You can't expect to live a logo-life and receive the branded profits. Real faith takes real work!

> *Then Jesus said to them, "Follow Me and I will make you become fishers of men." They immediately left their nets and followed Him.*
> **(Mark 1: 17-18)**

Imagine if some stranger came to your job and asked that you quit your job and follow Him. But that's exactly what Christ requires. He's asking you lay aside your life for His purpose. Christ doesn't want us to sacrifice our time; He wants us to sacrifice our life. So why don't we?

The real reason is because we think that we're living for ourselves. We consider this small time on Earth and end up sacrificing our entire Eternity. God is calling people just like you to reach people that others wouldn't even think about. Just think about it, if you have problems with drugs and alcohol, who would you rather listen to: a minister telling you about your sin or a minister with a testimony of how he overcame drugs and alcohol himself? Don't despise the path that the Lord allowed you to travel, those were just lessons for you to teach who God's made you to reach!

Luke 9:23 tells us that in order to follow Jesus, we must first deny ourselves. This is a tough one, because who wants to look in the mirror and tell themselves no? Denying yourself hurts! In order to follow Jesus, I have to spend more time with Him. In order to follow Jesus, I have to change the places that I hangout. In order to follow Jesus, so on and so on. Denial begins to sound like a list of unwanted rules. This is where your commitment to Christ comes in. If you're going to follow Christ, you have to know WHY you are following Him! What makes you seek Christ when everything is going wrong in your life? What pushes you to seek Christ when you roll out of bed in the morning? What motivates you to get up and go to church 3 or 4 days a week? What is it?

When I found myself straddling the fence of Christianity, I realized that there was this void in me that I had long since been trying to fill. I was trying to fill it with ambition, goals, relationships, and whatever else I could. And no matter how successful I was in life, I was never really happy, always battling depression, always battling the fear of never being enough. It took me awhile, but after constant prayer and time with God, I realized that God loves me just as I am. I don't have to be a certain thing or look a certain way for Him to accept me. And even in my faults, He found favor in me, and that's when my whole life changed. I threw myself into pursuing God with all of my heart and all of my mind. All of a sudden, God's do's and don'ts didn't seem so demanding. I actually wanted to keep

His law, because I had begun to fall in love with Christ as my Savior.

I've said all that to say this, when you know why you follow Christ, you'll gladly lay down your life for Christ.

Prayer for being the brand

Dear Lord,

Help me to live for You

Day in and Day out.

Teach me what it means

To serve like You,

To sacrifice like You,

To be like You,

And to love like You.

Thank you Lord

For taking me this far,

And please, keep guiding me day by day.

Lord, help my living

To be an example for others

Seeking You.

In Jesus' name,

Amen.

Chapter 5:
A Diamond in the Rough

You were bought with a price, and you're worth every penny!

Get this fact, Jesus, God's son, left heaven for you. He traded in streets paved with gold for trashy dirt roads. He traded in a mansion for a shack which didn't even have an indoor bathroom. Jesus walked on Earth for 33 years just so He could say, 'Where you're standing, I've already stood. I've gone without. I've been hungry. I've been counted out. I've been lied on. I've been talked about. I've already been there.' Jesus chose not only to live for you, but to die for you, and He would've done it even if you were the only one.

1 Peter 2:9 tells us that we are a chosen generation called to be a royal and holy people. God made us to reign. But often times, what actually happens is that we go through life simply existing and never really fulfilling our destiny in Christ. Nothing about you is a mistake. Nothing that you've been through was a waste. God is going to use everything that was meant to delay you to eventually propel you

if you'd only believe. You're not washed up. You're never too far gone. God is and has always been standing by your side just waiting to receive you. You're a true diamond in the rough. No matter the situation, tell yourself, 'I'm coming out, better than I was before.' I'm coming out of bondage. I'm coming out of low self-esteem. I'm coming out of depression. I'm coming out of feeling sorry for myself.

> *For the message of the cross is foolishness to those who are perishing, but to us who are being saved it is the power of God.*
> **(1 Corinthians 1:18)**

When you step out and become the person that God wants you to be, even you won't recognize yourself. God is going to do such a work in you that not even you will believe (Habakkuk 1:5). God will start stirring up gifts and hidden talents that you never knew you were capable of. How do I know this? Because it happened to me! When God begins to work in your life, don't become discouraged when other people react differently to you. Remember, God's word has power to those who choose life. But that's exactly the problem, not everyone chooses life. Some people unconsciously declare death in their own circumstances by refusing to make changes that will revitalize their life. The word of God won't change anyone who's not searching for it.

Prayer of My Coming out

Dear Lord,

I thank You for the places

That You've taken me.

Yes, it was hard, and sometimes

God it hurt.

But I know now that in the midst of my troubles,

You were healing my pain.

In the midst of my tears,

You were erasing all of my fears.

I love you God,

And I trust you with my life.

Please, every day, help me to be more like Christ.

In Jesus' name,

Amen

Chapter 6:
Because You're Worth it, Every Problem Serves a Purpose!

I remember studying about the Egyptians in my high school History class. In such a hot area, the people depended on the Nile River for support. The Nile was the main component in both raising crops used for food to eat and raising the products that they wished to sell. The Nile was also a vital tool in making clay, which they used to make buildings and sculptures. The Nile was the source of their income, their livelihood, and their way of life. But every once in a while, the Nile would do the unthinkable and flood. The overflowing waters would destroy their crops, damage their homes, and claim the lives of anyone who could not find shelter. Recovering from this type of devastation took ages. Getting out of the victim mode, the Egyptians decided to chart the times between each flooding occurrence. By figuring out the time frame between each flooding episode, the Egyptians began to prepare for such catastrophe. They noted that it would be 365 days in between floods. As crazy as it may be, they used one of the most terrible experiences to chart one of the most important things in today's time, THE CALENDAR! Who knew that some of the worst times in their lives would produce such a big benefit for us today?

I used to love this story as a child, because I could never figure out for the life of me, what caused them to go from helplessness to hopefulness? Then it occurred to me that not every devastation is meant to knock you down, sometimes it's used to push you forward. Romans 8:28 tells us that all things work for the good of those who love the Lord. In other words, not everything that comes your way is meant to break you. So many times we get caught in the pitfalls of life; the loss of a job, the death of a loved one, time spent behind bars, time spent living on the streets, the pain of trying to recover from an illness, etc. Regardless of the problem, you can't just lie down and stay hidden. If you want to see God's best, then you have to be willing to go through every test.

It's just like a baby trying to learn how to walk. Over and over again, the baby tries to stand and step, but time after time, the baby falls. Instead of giving up, the baby puts on another smile and tries again. But somewhere along the way, we as adults act as if we're afraid to try and try again. We count ourselves out before we even get a chance to step in the game. If you don't believe in yourself, no one else will.

Therefore take up the whole armor of God that you may be able to withstand in the evil day, and having done all, to stand. . .
(Ephesians 6:13)

The bylines in this scripture are so powerful to me, because it's saying with everything that's happened and all of the chaos surrounding me, I don't have to react to every situation; I don't have to work out my issues; I don't have to justify my righteous; all I have to do is stand. Because Jesus went to the cross and did His part, all I have to do is STAND, not fight, stand; not argue, stand; not worry, stand.

I've heard people say that they hate going to Holiness churches, because you can't leave without getting your exercise. Every five seconds, you're on your feet. But backtracking with my spiritual eye, I see why they do it; it's because standing is the highest praise. I've lost my job, but I can still stand up and say that God is good. I don't have any money in the bank, but I can still stand up and say that God supplies all of my needs. I've lost my child, but I can still stand up and say that the joy of the Lord is my strength. To be able to say statements like this is beyond understanding. That's how we know that the power of our testimony is built in our stance. You see, the enemy tried his best to break you, but all he was doing was allowing God room to make you!

You were worth the pain. You were worth the struggle. You were worth being counted out. You were worth being lied on. You were worth being talked about. You were worth God taking five minutes out of His day to sit down and personally coach you through your trials (telling you the places to go, telling you what to do next, telling you how to put things into perspective. . . . you were worth that).

I grew up playing basketball. I had this one coach that fussed at me day in and day out. I could never do anything right. She was always in my ear complaining about something that I was doing. And it was crazy to me, because I wasn't even a part of her starting five. One day after practice, I felt so discouraged that I mustered up the courage to tell her that I was quitting. She listened to me, politely waited until I finished, and then said, "That's not going to happen." Shocked, I stood up and looked at her. That's when she told me, 'I never waste my breath on a player without potential. I'll see you at practice!'

That's when it hit me; she wasn't treating the other players like she treated me, because she didn't see the same abilities in them that she saw in me. God does the same thing. Why else would He waste His time taking you through trials when He already knows that you're going to complain, without first having a purpose for you? Get this; God is not going to waste His time on you if He hasn't chosen you. That's why James said when trials come count it all joy (James 1:2), because he got the concept that trials are just God's way of taking you through the crash-course of Christian living. Don't fight the process!

This is why the Be-Attitudes are so important in the gospels. They're Jesus' way of giving us a few tips on how to overcome life's obstacles. In the midst of your circumstance, you have to keep declaring, 'Blessed are they. . . .' When you find it hard to get along with somebody, keep telling yourself, 'Blessed are those that are peacemakers . . . (Matthew 5:9).' When you're giving life all you've got and it's still not enough, keep telling yourself, 'Blessed are they who hunger now, for they shall be filled (Luke 6: 21).' When you find it hard to forgive someone who's mistreated you, keep telling yourself, 'Blessed are the merciful . . . (Matthew 5:7).' These attitudes are Jesus' way of reminding us daily how to turn one obstacle into a lifetime opportunity.

Jacob used his fight with the angel to obtain lifetime favor with God (Genesis 32:22-32). Joseph used the lessons that he learned as a slave to teach him how to manage the supplies that God gave him as a governor of Egypt (Genesis 39-42). David used his experience as a shepherd to teach him how to lead God's people as King (1st & 2nd Samuel). Paul used his solitude in prison to write most of the bible that we still know and use today. Know that no time, regardless of the circumstance, is a waste for God. Some of your biggest obstacles will produce some of your greatest blessings.

Prayer for Overcoming Obstacles

Dear Lord,

I want to thank You

For all that You've done for me

And all that you continue to do.

Thank You Lord for encouraging me

Through my hardest times.

Thank You God for being

My leaning post.

Lord, no matter how bad things were

You never left my side.

As I go through my day God,

Please help me to see the good

In every situation

In Jesus' Name,

Amen.

I really hope that you enjoyed reading this. .

May God continue to bless and keep each and every one of you!

Other Books By Tatiana Whigham

From Butterflies to Caterpillars

Lyrics From An Old Soul

www.ingramcontent.com/pod-product-compliance
Lightning Source LLC
Chambersburg PA
CBHW072115290426
44110CB00014B/1917